GOOD
CITIZENSHIP
FOR TODAY

GOOD CITIZENSHIP FOR TODAY

A MIND SET ON CIVIL VIRTUE

William E. Thrasher, Jr.

GOOD CITIZENSHIP FOR TODAY
A MIND SET ON CIVIL VIRTUE

King James Version (KJV)
Public Domain

New International Version (NIV)
Holy Bible, New International Version®, NIV® Copyright ©1973, 1978, 1984, 2011 by Biblica, Inc.® Used by permission. All rights reserved worldwide.

iUniverse books may be ordered through booksellers or by contacting:

iUniverse
1663 Liberty Drive
Bloomington, IN 47403
www.iuniverse.com
1-800-Authors (1-800-288-4677)

ISBN: 978-1-5320-5764-9 (sc)
ISBN: 978-1-5320-5765-6 (e)

Library of Congress Control Number: 2018910856

Print information available on the last page.

iUniverse rev. date: 11/15/2018

Contents

Dedication

This book is dedicated to the memory of my late father, whose wise counsel I sorely miss; my late mother who was always my greatest cheerleader; and my daughters, Tiffany, Willowry, Brittany, and Chelsey: my greatest treasures.

Foreword

William Thrasher, Jr. is one of my former high school students and a friend whom I have followed through his youth on into his professional work. His family background provided him with the capacity to treat people with respect, a sense of caring and love, making him "right" for leadership, guidance, and everyday fellowship, whether from the pulpit, the classroom, or every - day living. *Good Citizenship for Today* is a testament to both his parents and grandparents.

Upon reading *Good Citizenship for Today*, I was amazed at how skillfully William managed to quote from the many teachings and preaching of Jesus. He shows the reader the relationship to Good Citizenship, which grows from spiritual values, always pulling from truth, thoughts, and good behavior. Furthermore, inclusive in the book is the Good Citizenship for Today User Guide which William challenges the reader of this remarkable booklet to transform teaching and counseling principles into practical goal oriented outcomes, including lesson plans and measurable results.

William seems to be profoundly aware of the meaning of American constitutional democracy — self-knowledge, literacy and responsibility for the beloved community, which Dr. Martin Luther King, Jr. often spoke and preached about.

William touched ever so softly upon individual and group dynamics, including individual rights versus the rights of the group and that of course, so often creates conflicts in our institutions and legal systems. Again, William dug into the economic and social divide among socioeconomic classes, and political groups.

William raises the right questions, stating the problem faced in our individual, family and group living.

I am confident that the reader will find William's book useful and practical. Done with simplicity and insight, presented with profound and lasting biblical and poetic allusions, Good Citizenship for Today is a remarkable achievement.

Dr. Morris Holmes

Former Superintendent of Orleans Parish School Board, Little Rock School District and Principal of the Historical Landmark Little Rock Central High School

From the Author

When I was a child, my parents taught my brothers and sisters and me that, while good grades in the "Three R's" were important, nothing less than an "A" in citizenship would be acceptable. That rule applied from kindergarten through twelfth grade. My, how times have changed! We now live in a world that has become too fast and too furious. Society as we know it has become quite self-centered. The Golden Rule, "Do unto others as you would have them do unto you," has been transformed into the Gold Rule, "He who has the gold makes the rules." In a large segment of our society, more emphasis is placed on the size of one's bank account than the size of one's character. While some in society seem to overlook bad behavior, a growing segment of society resents those who believe that, for whatever the reason, the rule of law does not apply to them. Often, those who maintain inflated ideas about their own importance are the ones who fall into this mind set. This little book is designed to speak to not only those who share this way of thinking, but anyone who wants to rise above the eschewed, self-centered "I/me" mentality. While the Screen Bean caricatures are meant to flirt with your imagination, the subject matter is meant to arouse inner thoughts regarding good citizenship. Good citizenship is more than a concept; it is the responsibility of all people in society.

Civil virtue is the fruit of good citizenship. *Star Trek's* Commander Spock said that "the needs of the many outweigh the needs of the one." Whatever is in the best interest of the community is more important than the desires of any one individual. Good citizens should always consider the welfare of their communities in contrast with their personal desires. Communities are stronger because their members are stronger. Whenever people work together for the common good, civil virtue flourishes.

To Be or Not To Be?

"To be or not to be?" was the resounding question posed by Shakespeare's Hamlet. The answer for those striving for good citizenship is "To Be".

There is an adage asserting that one's *altitude*, the height to which one can soar towards achievement, is determined by one's *attitude*, how one presents himself, as well as how one treats others. The following are "To Be's" that have stood the test of time as the best representations of attitudes that lead to civil virtue.

Be Poor in Spirit

To be poor in spirit means to be humble. Christ once said, "He who humbles himself shall be exalted" (Luke 18:14). The value of humility is priceless. When one humbles oneself, he opens the door of abundant opportunity. Being humble means that a person realizes that they don't have all of the answers and that they recognize the need to be open to ideas from others.

A truck driver once got his 18-wheeler truck stuck under a bridge. While he pondered his dilemma, a young boy happened along and observed his situation. "Hey Mister," the boy said, "I can tell you how to get your truck unstuck." The driver waved the youngster off and told him to go away. The driver called the local transportation department for assistance. Inspectors, architects and civil engineers arrived on the scene. None could determine a proper, cost-effective way to remove the truck. The little boy remained nearby, watching the men and women scratch their heads. He approached the group and repeated yet again that he had the answer to their problem. Amused, one of the engineers suggested that they listen to the young man, since they themselves had not arrived at any useful solutions. "All you have to do," the boy said, "is let some air out of the tires." The truck driver, had he shown a little humility in the beginning and listened to the boy, could have solved his dilemma in a matter of minutes. Humility is one of the characteristics of good citizenship.

Be Mournful

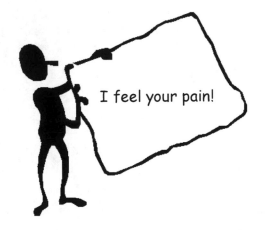

To be mournful means to be empathetic toward the suffering of others. Walk in their shoes, feel their pain, suffer with them. Bear one another's burdens. The biblical story of the "Good Samaritan" is a great example of such behavior.

There once was a man who was met with great misfortune. On his way to town to conduct business, he was met by some thieves who held him up, beat him and left him for dead. Three of his own countrymen saw him and they ignored him. A man from Samaria, a land outside the injured man's community, happened to be traveling along the road and saw the man's plight. Samaritans were not respected in the victim's homeland. The Samaritan carried the man to safety and paid some local citizens to care for the injured man. He told them he would return to check on the man's welfare and would provide further assistance if needed. The "Good Samaritan" put the needs of the injured man before his own. Thus, this parable has been a timeless lesson in the practice of good citizenship.

Be Meek

"The Meek shall inherit the earth" Jesus declared in Matthew 5. There are those who think that to be meek means to be weak or afraid. Truthfully speaking, it takes more courage to be meek than to be an aggressor. When Christ said, "turn the other cheek", He was not saying be afraid and cower. Instead, He was encouraging us to be bold and do the hard thing: rise above our basic instincts to render evil for evil. Meekness means that you don't intimidate others. You don't use your personal might to get your way. Isaac Asimov, one of the twentieth century's premier science fiction writers, once said "Violence is the last refuge of the incompetent." People who would rather fight than find peaceful solutions to conflict are people who have a very limited view of themselves and their value. Humans are all precious in God's sight and should recognize one another's value. Meekness is a quality of civil virtue.

Be Hungry & Thirsty
For Righteousness

A person should hunger for what is morally right. It is beneficial to search out individuals whose integrity and good reputations can be emulated. Psalm 37:37 says it best: "Mark the perfect man and behold the upright: for the end of that man is peace." Be earnest when searching for a role model. Seek the individual whose life is not chaotic and who wears good citizenship like a coat of armor. Observe them as they tackle life's challenges with dignity and respect. See how they treat others despite fortune or social status. Drink from their well of wisdom and the thirst for civil virtue will be quenched.

Be Merciful

To be merciful means to be forgiving. It means to be understanding, to be patient with others' shortcomings. The American playwright Wilson Mizner once said, "Be nice to people on your way up because you'll meet them on your way down."

How one approaches others in society is akin to planting seeds. If one sows the seeds of disrespect or abuse, one cannot anticipate a harvest of good will. This concept cycles back to the earlier reference to the "Golden Rule". As a good citizen, one cannot be more virtuous than when exercising love of one's neighbor.

Be Pure In Heart

To be pure in heart means to harbor no malice or bad thoughts against others. It means not to be jealous or envious of others and to wish them only the best.

It is important to experience the power of goodness and to bathe in the radiance of virtue for its own sake. In Psalm 73, the Psalmist becomes weary because, on the surface, it appears his goodness is being overshadowed by the irreverence and bad behavior of others. When he seeks the solace of the sanctuary, he finds that bad behavior ends with dire consequences and that the fruits of a pure heart are everlasting.

There is a myth that asserts good guys always finish last. This is the rhetoric of those without virtue. Good citizenship is its own reward and never finishes last.

Be a Peacemaker

To be a peacemaker means to do the utmost to maintain calm and order around you. Be slow to offend, but quick to bring peace to chaotic situations. Agree to disagree with your adversary. The fastest way to trouble is to go looking for it. In the American Old West, a gunfighter's reputation and his very life hinged on him being the fastest to draw his weapon. Eventually there would be someone who was faster. His prospects for a great future were never good. In *The New Living Translation of the Bible*, Psalm 34:14 reads, "Turn from evil and do good. Search for peace and work to maintain it." Good citizens know that peace is worth working for and virtue is its reward.

Be Persecuted for Doing The Right Thing.

To be persecuted for doing the right thing means to be willing to take an unpopular stand for that which you know to be right, even if you must stand alone. The lyrics from the song "The Impossible Dream", from Broadway's *Man of La Mancha*, highlight such a stance: "To fight for the right without question or pause/to be willing to march into hell for a Heavenly cause…." Standing up for what one believes to be morally right may require great personal sacrifice. An unpopular stance can subject a person to public ridicule or ostracism. Can this be a sort of test of one's civic virtue? Of course. Good citizens routinely subject themselves to such challenges in order to effect change for the better in society.

Be an ELI

Eli is an acronym for "Encourage, Lift, and Inspire".

An Eli is one who encourages others, lifts up others who may be otherwise downtrodden and inspires others to be their personal best. The apostle Paul's words in 1 Corinthians 9:22 serve to galvanize such social practices: "I have become all things to all people that I might by all means save some."

Modern youth are bombarded with peer pressure that frequently leads to bullying and other forms of abuse. Such negative behaviors can only be countered with examples of the opposite conduct. Encourage those who lack self-confidence; lift up those who may have stumbled in human error and inspire those who yearn to do more or become more than their current circumstances seem to allow. Jesus declared in John 8:12 that we are the "light of the world" and, in turn, humanity lives in that light. When we are Elis, the light shines brighter. Good citizens should all be Elis.

Show Love to Others

"Even though I speak in every human and angelic language and have not love in my heart, I am no better than echoing bronze or the clash of cymbals." 1 Corinthians 13

Good citizenship requires that you show love to others. Love your neighbor as you love yourself. Good citizenship is not a practice one can fake; it is action that reflects your true nature. Self-esteem is revealed in how one treats others. Living by the example of showing love will reveal what love can do.

- Love is patient
- Love is kind.
- Love does not envy.
- Love does not boast.
- Love is not proud.
- Love is not rude.
- Love is not self-seeking.
- Love is slow to anger.
- Love does not keep score of others' wrongs.
- Love dislikes evil but celebrates the truth.
- Love always protects.
- Love always trusts.
- Love always hopes.
- Love always perseveres.

Love never fails. (1Corinthians 13)

To summarize, love knows no boundaries, nor has any limitations when it comes to how one treats others. Love is resilient; it can be bent, stretched, and twisted out of shape, but it cannot be broken. Its source is all-powerful. Every good citizen wills this power and is a formidable force for good.

Get A New Outlook On Life

The world should not shape one's thoughts or outlook on life. It is important to open our minds to the transforming power of new ideas. By opening one's mind, one gains access to life's limitless possibilities.

Good citizenship is often influenced by world opinion. There was a time when mankind thought the world was flat. As colossal a mistake as that was, there are yet as many inaccurate opinions in the modern world that have a negative effect on our society. For instance, the popular perception that drug use is "cool" or "hip" causes infinite social problems. Substances that alter our ability to think clearly or ultimately destroy human lives are not supporting a healthy and productive society.

To be a good citizen, one must preserve a clear mind in order to see the truth. Our outlook dictates our behavior. If a person's ability to know and see the truth is inhibited, then that person will live in a lie. They will promote more lies. Lies handcuff us, restricting our freedom to be good citizens. Truth, and our clear grasp of it, sets us free.

Think Good Thoughts

"…Whatever is true, whatever is noble, whatever is right, whatever is pure, whatever is lovely, whatever is admirable, if anything is excellent or praiseworthy—think about such things" (Philippians 4:8).

There is an old computer-programming expression "Junk in, junk out." It means that if the input into the computer is junk, then the output will be the same. The same is true with one's mind. If a person constantly internalizes negative thoughts, then negative behavior will be the outcome. Good citizenship requires positive, healthy thoughts about oneself and others. Here are some concepts to ponder:

- Truth: It is liberating.
- Nobility: It is the quality of being honorable and dignified.
- Righteousness: It is the quality of being just.
- Purity: It is to have a character that is spotless or without blemish.
- Loveliness: It makes one endearing and amiable.
- Admiration: It is the way in which people view your just and honorable self.
- Excellence: It is the high ideal toward which one should aspire to be virtuous and worthy of praise.

Paul summarized this best in the book of Philippians: "…Whatever is true, whatever is noble, whatever is right, whatever is pure, whatever is lovely, and whatever is admirable, if anything, is excellent or praiseworthy." We must cherish these concepts. Good citizens should embrace and display these qualities.

Think on The Value of Truth

Traditionally, when we think of truth we think of it in a legal sense: "the truth, the whole truth, and nothing but the truth." Truth is liberating at times in a legal venue. Lies compromise integrity and become a ball and chain that weighs a person down. "You shall know the truth; only the truth shall set you free" (John 8:32). Thierry Maertens, O.S.B., in his book *Bible Themes Volume 1* explores truth from a deeper, more spiritual perspective. He states that truth is a matter of fidelity, insofar as one's capacity to be relied upon. E.F. Hutton, the nation's oldest brokerage, once had a marketing slogan: "When E. F. Hutton talks, people listen." It is important for a person to have the credibility that makes people listen, and believe them, when they speak. Speaking truth sustains a person's honor as a good citizen.

To use another example, Aesop's fable "The Boy Who Cried Wolf" is emblematic of the value of truth from two perspectives. The subject of the story, a shepherd boy, is a practical joker who loves to be the center of attention in his community. He would become bored watching over the sheep and would amuse himself by crying "Wolf!", just to make the townspeople run to his aid. One day, a wolf actually does attack the flock, but when the shepherd boy cries out, no one will come. The wolf attacks the sheep and kills them, and the boy returns to his village, weeping, asking the townspeople why no one came to his aid. He is told that no one believes a liar. The boy's lies were his own undoing. Good citizenship means speaking the truth always, so that others can rely on one's word.

Think Noble Thoughts

To think noble thoughts means to contemplate engaging in activities that will benefit the welfare of your fellow man. Consider becoming active in your community, doing things like volunteering some of your time with community organizations that feed the hungry, work with the elderly, or that work with the underprivileged. By acting on those thoughts, you develop into the good citizen whom you aspire to be.

Right Thinking Is the Key

"Happy is the man who does not take the wicked for his guide, nor walk the road that the wicked tread, nor sits in the company of the insolent, but whose greatest pleasure is in the law of the Lord. And, in His law does he study day and night" (Psalm 1).

Always be mindful of the company you keep. Bad company yields bad results—in other words, trouble. A person's character can be defined by the company they keep, i.e. the people with whom they surround themselves. Christ said: "You can tell a tree by the fruit that it bears" (Matthew 7:16). The key to good citizenship is to bear fruit that will benefit mankind.

Pure Thoughts Are Priceless!

Pure thoughts are like flawless, precious gems. What makes a precious gem priceless is time and pressure. Pure thoughts are made priceless by time and experience.

Have you ever asked yourself what motivates you? Why do you do the things that you do? Our motives say a lot about how we think. Is money the only factor that drives you? Is praise for what you do the key, or is it a matter of doing the right thing for its own sake? Pure thoughts are not selfish. Pure thoughts dictate actions that are not motivated by greed, but by a sense of what is right. Pure thoughts promote good deeds.

Lovely Thoughts Are Crystalized

Lovely thoughts are like diamonds waiting to come forth. If you can crystallize the beautiful thoughts that fill your mind and heart, you can bring these thoughts to fruition. Crystalized thoughts make things happen.

The great pyramids of Egypt began as ideas before they were constructed and became realities—as were the Eiffel Tower, the Empire State Building, Mt. Rushmore and so forth. Is there a gem of thought inside you longing to emerge into something great? When a person focuses on a lovely, crystalized thought, that thought, or idea, will lead him or her forward in everything they do. The people one meets while moving forward will also help to bring the sparkling jewel of an idea into the light, making it a shining reality.

Think Admirable
Thoughts of Others

When one sees the light of goodness shining in others, good citizenship dictates that one should show appreciation. Sometimes a kind word is all that is needed when we see others struggling. If you see good work going unnoticed, say something! Let that person or persons know that you value their sacrifice. This is what good citizens do.

Excellence in Thought
is Illuminating

Excellent thoughts signify that a person has high ideals. High ideals are illuminating. Excellent thoughts translate into illuminating actions.

Excellence is like a bright light in a dark room. Good citizenship is excellence at its best. There is something divine about allowing the excellence that resides within us to illuminate those around us. Christ would say "Ye are the light of the world… let your light shine before men, that they may see your good works and glorify your father which is in heaven" (Matthew 5:15-16).

Good Citizenship Is
A Work of Art

When we summarize all the concepts and practices behind what it takes to be a good citizen, it becomes clear that a person can paint their own picture of the good citizen they wish to be. Truth, nobility, righteousness, purity, loveliness, appreciation and excellence embody a true work of art.

See Yourself As
A Role Model

As a practitioner of good citizenship, a person should be a shining example of what is right. In so doing, the world will see the divine inspiration behind a person's actions. It is said that imitation is the highest form of flattery. If that is true, live so that others will want to be like you. Respect yourself. It is difficult to show respect to others when you don't respect yourself. When you feel good about yourself, it is easy for others to see it.

In the mid- to late '90s, Michael Jordan was such a dominant force on the basketball court that a whole generation of kids wanted to "be like Mike." Not everyone can play basketball like Michael Jordan, but they can be the best that they can be in their own aspirations.

Envision yourself as the best example of a friend to mankind and others will beat a path to your door to be just like you!

Remember How You Got There

"Therefore, since such a great cloud of witnesses surrounds us, let us throw off everything that hinders and the sin that so easily entangles, and let us run with perseverance the race marked out for us" (Hebrews 12:1).

All too often success breeds forgetfulness. It is important to remember that there were many who sacrificed so that our success could be possible. We stand on the shoulders of those who came before us. Without that foundation beneath, our success would not have been possible.

Remember also that "to whom much is given, much is required" (Luke 12:48). We must also make sacrifices for those who come behind us. We must set aside the things that might hinder our progress or cause us to stumble in the race carved out for us. We must persevere, determined to succeed not only for our sakes, but for the sake of future generations.

Learn How to Laugh

"A merry heart is good medicine, but a crushed spirit dries up the bones" (Proverbs 17:22).

Just like flowers need rain for nourishment, they also need sunshine to grow. We are no different. Our souls need a good laugh. Laughter is sunshine for the soul. It's like medicine for an aching spirit. A person can't be serious all the time. Nobody likes a grouch, but that's what one becomes with no laughter in his or her life. Every now and then, it's important to lighten up.

This does not mean laughter at the expense of others. It does, however, mean that at times you must laugh at yourself. When you can learn how to laugh at yourself, to not take yourself so seriously, that's when you know that you have become tolerant of others. A sense of humor is an important key to good citizenship.

Lend A Helping Hand

Matthew 5:41 states "whoever compels you to go one mile, go with him two." Give to the one that asks of you; do not turn away from the one who wants to borrow from you.

Remember the story of the Good Samaritan? A man had been beaten and left for dead. Two of the man's own countrymen passed him by, but a Samaritan, who should have passed him by, stopped, picked him up, took him to get help, and made sure that all his needs were met. The Samaritan paid no mind to sect, cult, or color when he saw the man. He saw a fellow human being, in need of help.

A person who never needs help is probably a lonely person. The 16th century English poet John Donne wrote that "No man is an island." Humans are together on earth to help one another. It is critical for the social good that we help our neighbors. We never know when we ourselves may be in need. Take the time, go the distance, and humanity will be better for it. Generosity and charity are elements of good citizenship.

Don't Quit

In a race, many runners participate, but only one will get the prize. It's important to remember that it is the way a race is run that defines the outcome.

Life is like a race. Not everyone who starts the race will finish at the same time. Some will be faster; some will be slower. We must learn that the race will not be won by the person who is fastest. The race of life is about endurance. In Aesop's fable "The Hare and the Tortoise", the Hare is expected to win the race, because of his swiftness of foot. The Hare took his speed and agility for granted and so he took his time, napping and loitering about. The Tortoise in the meantime kept his eye on the finish line, and though he was slow, he was steady: he crossed the finish line first. The key is to keep running, no matter what *Don't quit!* No matter how hard the trial, *don't quit!* No matter how exhausting the struggle, *don't quit.* No matter how difficult the task, *don't quit!* You must remain determined if you want to win the prize. Sir Winston Churchill gave a commencement address to one of the graduating classes at Oxford University and the following is the address in its entirety: "Never, never, never, never, never, never, never give up."

Anger Management

"In your anger, do not sin. Do not let the sun go down while you are still angry" (Ephesians 4:26).

The proverbial "they" always asserts that there are two things in life that cannot be avoided: death and taxes. Somehow, "they" manage to overlook anger. Anger is a natural human emotion that everyone experiences at some point. While there are times we know in advance that someone or something is going to push our anger button, anger can sneak up on us when we least expect it. Since anger cannot be avoided, it is up to us to control it, rather than vice versa. Some folks say count to ten; others say go to that pleasant place in your mind. Another option is to examine the source of our anger and ask ourselves what we can do to change the circumstances without doing harm to anyone, including one's self. Anger that lingers past sundown can take control of a person. Anger management is a civil virtue and a facet of good citizenship.

Value Your Conversation

"The tongue that brings healing is a tree of life, but a deceitful tongue crushes the spirit" (Proverbs 15:4).

Sticks and stones may break our bones, but harsh words can hurt as well. They can sometimes do more harm than physical damage. You are not defiled by what goes in you, but rather by what comes out. If your conversation is rude and disrespectful, your credibility will suffer. If your conversation is foul or vulgar, your credibility will suffer. "By your words, you will be justified; by your words, you will be condemned" (Matthew 12:37). "A soft word turns away wrath, but a harsh word stirs up anger" (Proverbs 15:1). To value your conversation means to refrain from speaking harsh words, but instead speak gentle words of peace. "Gracious words are like a honeycomb: sweetness to the soul and health to the body" (Proverbs 16:24). At all times we must exemplify civil virtue as a good citizen should.

Don't Judge

"Do not judge, or you, too, will be judged. For in the same way you judge others, you will be judged; with the measure you use, it will be measured to you" (Matthew 7:1-2).

All too often people are judged by their differences, rather than the content of their character. Our uniqueness makes humanity special. To say that one is better or worse based on race, sex, creed or color or any other cultural difference is to make the same mistake that bigots throughout history have made. Make room for others and their uniqueness and room will be made for yours. Martin Luther King, in his "I Have a Dream" speech, stated that he dreamt of a day when men would be judged by the "content of their character" rather than the color of their skin. When a person displays good citizenship, civil virtue comes alive.

If Not You, Then Who?

In his famous inauguration address, President John F. Kennedy posed a very provocative challenge to the American people: "Ask not what your country can do for you—ask what you can do for your country."

Good citizenship is not something that can be passed off to someone else. The buck stops with us. We should ask ourselves each day what we can do to practice good citizenship. We are all responsible for our own civil virtue.

Where Do I Start?

The first step towards good citizenship is the most important one. You must commit to it. You commit to it by affirming the following:

I will treat others as I want to be treated.
I will seek peace and embrace it.
I will love my neighbor as I love myself.
I will be a willing servant to all mankind.
I will think and act with positive determination.
I will be slow to anger, but quick with patience.
I will laugh more and share good cheer.
I will elevate the quality of my conversation.
I will be a shining example of Good Citizenship.

Certificate of Good Citizenship

This Certificate of Good Citizenship is awarded to
_____*on this* _____*day*
*of*_____*for outstanding*
commitment to the principles of good citizenship and
For exhibiting those characteristics throughout his/her
Community and all mankind.

Good Citizenship
For Today
A Mind Set on Civil Virtue
User Guide

Good Citizenship For Today User Guide

The key to a good learning experience begins with the right environment. Teachers challenged with the added responsibility of dealing with excessive behavioral problems spend at minimum 50% of their time dealing with those issues, which leaves very little time for teaching. **The Good Citizenship for Today Rewards Program** is designed to provide educators with a provocative, dynamic tool for encouraging students to exhibit good behavior.

Each student will be issued a copy of the booklet for which the program is entitled, **Good Citizenship for Today.** At the beginning of the program the students who participate will be asked to sign a contract acknowledging their commitment to the program. At the end of the school year those students who have exhibited good behavior will receive a certificate of good citizenship as shown in the back of their book.

Along with the booklet, teachers will be provided this user guide that will offer effective activities that the students can engage in to further instill the importance of good behavior in general and in the classroom in particular.

Students who sign on for the program will receive a Star

for each week of the grading period and at the end of the semester they will receive a Semester Seal of Approval. Pizza parties are suggested as 9 week or semester incentive rewards. A 9 week wall of fame for Good Citizens is recommended to further encourage the students to stay on task. At the end of the School year they will receive the Official Good Citizenship Seal distinguishing them as outstanding Good Citizens. The Seals will be Gold, Silver, and Bronze. Gold Seals represent nine Stars per semester. Silver Seals eight and Bronze seven. Those students who receive the seals will be acknowledged at the schools special assembly along with the schools other awards.

Support for the Good Citizenship for Today Reward Program will come from local church groups and Parental involvement organizations, along with corporate sponsors. The local church groups will serve as "Adopters" of the program that will provide mentors for the students. The parental involvement organizations will be responsible for securing parents support for the program and the corporate sponsors will be asked to provide snacks such as pizza, burgers, and beverages as part of the incentive awards.

Additional support for the program will be sought after through grants and other funding sources committed to the cause of instilling the principals of Good Citizenship which ultimately yields a quality education for our youth.

Contract of Commitment

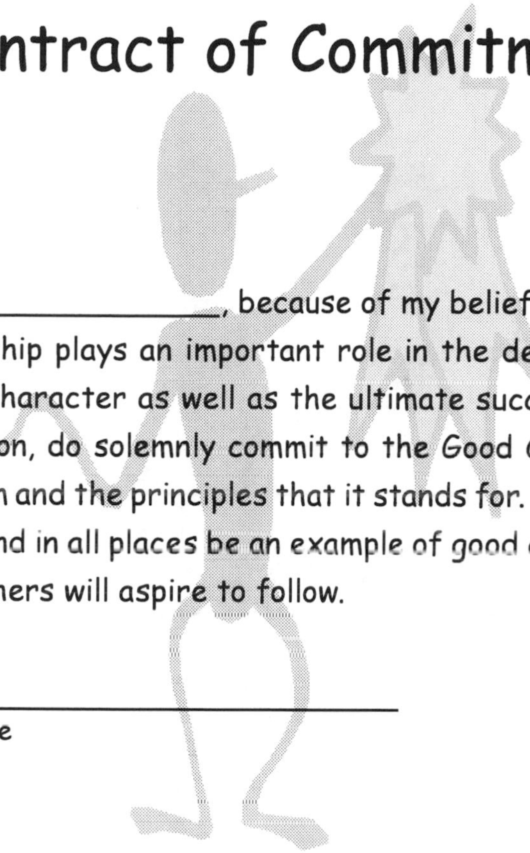

I _____, because of my belief that good citizenship plays an important role in the development of my character as well as the ultimate success of my education, do solemnly commit to the Good Citizenship Program and the principles that it stands for. I will at all times and in all places be an example of good citizenship that others will aspire to follow.

_____

Signature

_____

Date

This Certificate of Good Citizenship is awarded to
_____*on this* _____*day*
*of*_____*for outstanding*
commitment to the principles of good citizenship and
For exhibiting those characteristics throughout his/her
Community and all mankind.

Suggested Activities List

1. Volunteer at local community centers

2. Volunteer at church sponsored community organizations.

3. Make a wall of fame at each local church for students who are participating in the program.

4. Participates in team sponsored debates dealing with relevant subject matter.

5. Write essays on the importance of Good Citizenship citing community leaders that they believe best exemplify good citizenship.

6. Choose one of the caricatures from the book that best reflects their idea of good citizenship and write a short story, a poem or rap and or a play about it.

7. Create a group for those students who successfully finish the program.

8. Have inexpensive pins made up to pin on each program participant.

9. Have the local churches adopt the school where their children attend and notify the school that their children are participating in the program. Further, have the school counselor or vice principle keep the church up to date on how well each student is faring (behavior wise) that is participating in the program, in case there needs to be intervention by the church.

10. Send photos and articles to the local news papers recognizing the successful participants.

Printed in the United States
By Bookmasters